POLICE RESCUE

Deborah Chancellor

This edition 2015

First published in 2012 by
Franklin Watts
338 Euston Road
London, NW1 3BH

Franklin Watts Australia
Level 17/207 Kent Street
Sydney, NSW 2000

A CIP catalogue record for this book
is available from the British Library

Dewey Classification: 629.2'25
ISBN: 978 1 4451 3813 8

Printed in China

Series editors Adrian Cole/Amy Stephenson
Editor: Sarah Ridley
Art direction: Peter Scoulding
Designer: Steve Prosser
Picture researcher: Diana Morris

Franklin Watts is a division of
Hachette Children's Books,
an Hachette UK company.
www.hachette.co.uk

Contents

Fast car

Police cars race to the scene of a crime.
Sirens scream and bright lights flash.

WHEEOOO!

Police officers do not always
drive fast. When they **patrol**
an area they drive more slowly.

Police officers use a small computer to check information with the police central computer.

POLICE

1558

Slow down

A police traffic control car chases the fastest vehicles on the road. Its sirens can be heard a long way away.

WHOOEE! WHOOEE!

The police car has a built-in **camera**.
This can film dangerous drivers.

The car's
radar and **laser**
equipment is used

Top speed

BRRRRMM!
BRRRRMM!

A police motorbike zooms through narrow streets and traffic jams to be first at an emergency.

BEEEEEP!
BEEEEEP!

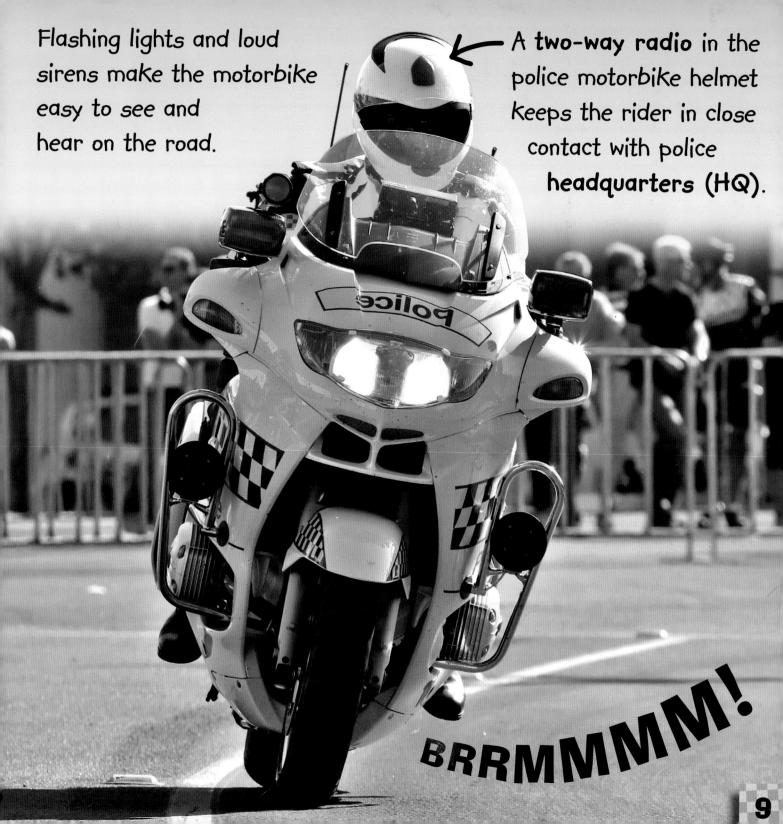

Flashing lights and loud sirens make the motorbike easy to see and hear on the road.

A **two-way radio** in the police motorbike helmet keeps the rider in close contact with police headquarters (HQ).

BRRMMMM!

9

Bumpy trip

Police quad bikes carry police officers over beaches and across hillsides. Wide tyres make the ride less bumpy.

WOOF!

BRRRRMM! BRRRRMM!

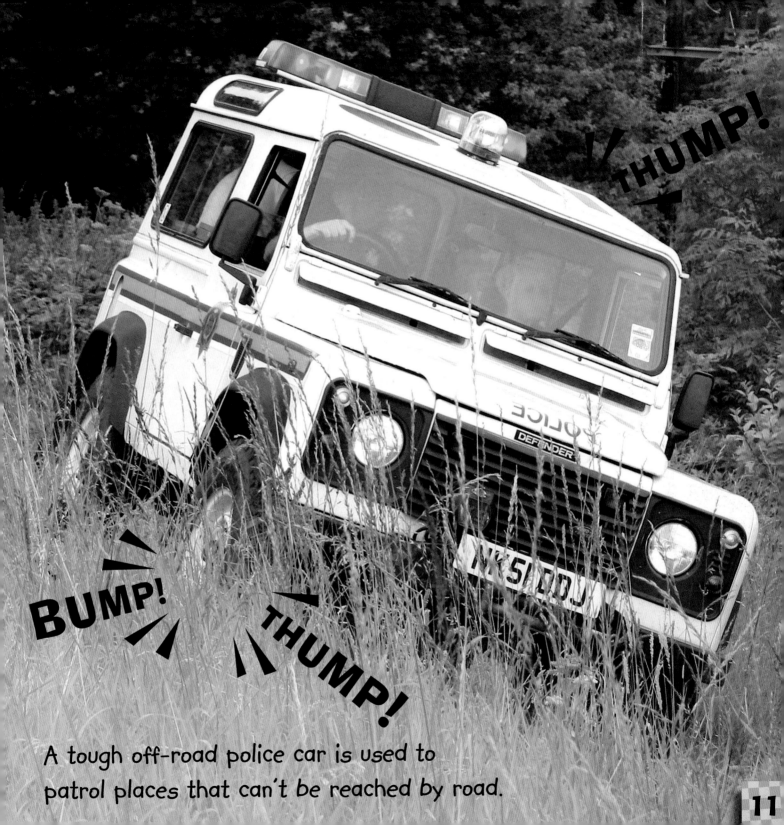

A tough off-road police car is used to
patrol places that can't be reached by road.

Back-up

POLICE

A strong police back-up van transports equipment, prisoners or police officers from one place to another.

The sides of a police van are strengthened to protect it. A flip-down shield stops anything from smashing the windscreen.

POLICE

POLICE

OU08 EEV

BEEEEP! BEEEEP!

Bright markings show that this is a police van.

Spy in the sky

A noisy police helicopter hovers above an **incident** on the ground. It gives back-up for crowd control and high-speed car chases.

WHUPPPA!

CHUPPPA!

CHUPPPA!

WHUPPPA!

Cameras are used to keep watch on a **suspect**.

The helicopter's heat-seeking camera senses a person's body heat or a vehicle's engine heat.

This allows the camera to track the smallest movements on the ground.

Search and rescue

WHUPPA! CHUPPA!

Police air ambulances look for people who are lost or in danger. They can fly injured or sick people straight to hospital.

WHUPPPA! CHUPPPA!

Searchlights and **tracking technology** help helicopters to work at night.

Water patrol

This police boat patrols rivers, **harbours** and coastal waters. It has sirens and flashing lights to warn other boats to let it pass.

Police boats have powerful motors, so they can speed through choppy waters.

Radar is used to track and follow suspects.

BRUMM!

SPLASH!

WHOOSHH!

SPLASH!

POLICE

Snow trek

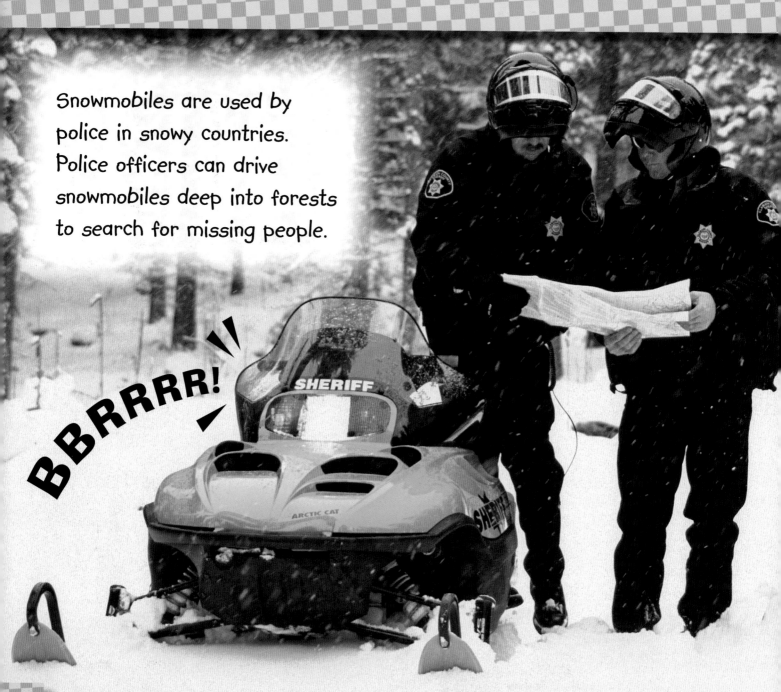

Snowmobiles are used by police in snowy countries. Police officers can drive snowmobiles deep into forests to search for missing people.

BBRRRR!

SHERIFF

ARCTIC CAT

SHERIFF

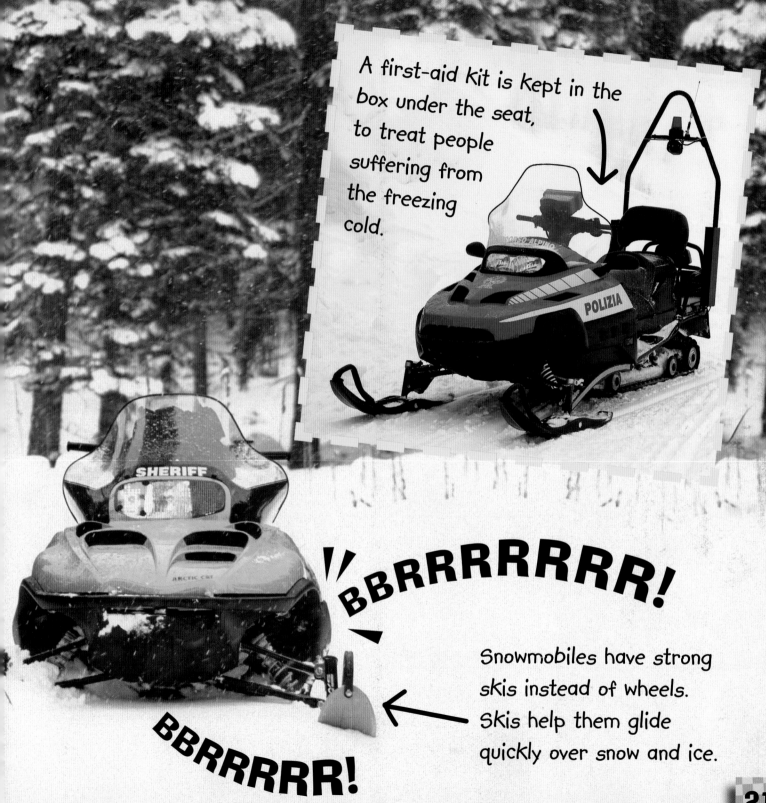

A first-aid kit is kept in the box under the seat, to treat people suffering from the freezing cold.

POLIZIA

SHERIFF

ARCTIC CAT

BBRRRRRRR!

BBRRRRR!

Snowmobiles have strong skis instead of wheels. Skis help them glide quickly over snow and ice.

Glossary

camera
police vehicles and helicopters use cameras to film suspects. Heat-seeking cameras sense movement when it is dark

harbour
a place where boats go to shelter or unload their goods

headquarters (HQ)
the most important police station in an area

incident
an event, either a crime or an emergency

laser
equipment that records how fast something is going

patrol
to check an area for possible problems

radar
equipment that finds out where another car, boat or plane is

siren
a loud hooting or wailing noise

suspect
someone who may have committed a crime

tracking technology
gadgets that help find and follow someone or something

two-way radio
a radio set you use to talk with somebody far away

Quiz

1. Do all police cars drive fast?

2. Why do the police use motorbikes?

3. What is special about a police motorbike helmet?

4. Why do the police need off-road vehicles?

5. What are police helicopters for?

6. Why do police boats have sirens?

Index

WEEOOW!